Road to Dreamland

AN ADVENTURE INTO PAEDIATRIC ANAESTHESIA

Written by Lara Veronese
Illustrated by Amanda Letcher

For my special family

Illustrations by Amanda Letcher

ISBN: 978-0-646-73032-5 (hardcover)
ISBN: 978-0-646-73098-1 (paperback)

Your Dreamland Explorer instructions

First, snuggle in and read the whole story from start to finish.
Feel the wonder, meet the Dream Machine and get ready for your next mission!
Now it's time to read again and take on your Dreamland Explorer Challenges:

The Great Animal Escape

Oh no! Some animals have escaped from Dreamland and are hiding in the hospital. Can you spot the following: Koala, Monkey, Butterfly, Giraffe, Elephant, Crocodile, Hippo.

Hungry Tummy Challenge

Kids waiting for surgery are often hungry.
Can you spy the following: Strawberry, Pineapple, Banana, Icecream, Iceblock, Cherry, Pear, Juice box.

Secret Code Hunt

Hidden on each page is a polka-dot letter or two. Write them all down and, at the end, use them to unlock a secret message.

Real-Life Hospital Quest

At the end of this book, there's a list of real things you might see in a hospital. See how many you can spot in the story and if you visit a hospital, ask your anaesthetist to help you find and tick them off!

The road to Dreamland

is full of smiles,

Where nurses and doctors

go extra miles!

First, you'll find a remote-controlled table for a bed,

Next, a squishy donut cushion cradles your head.

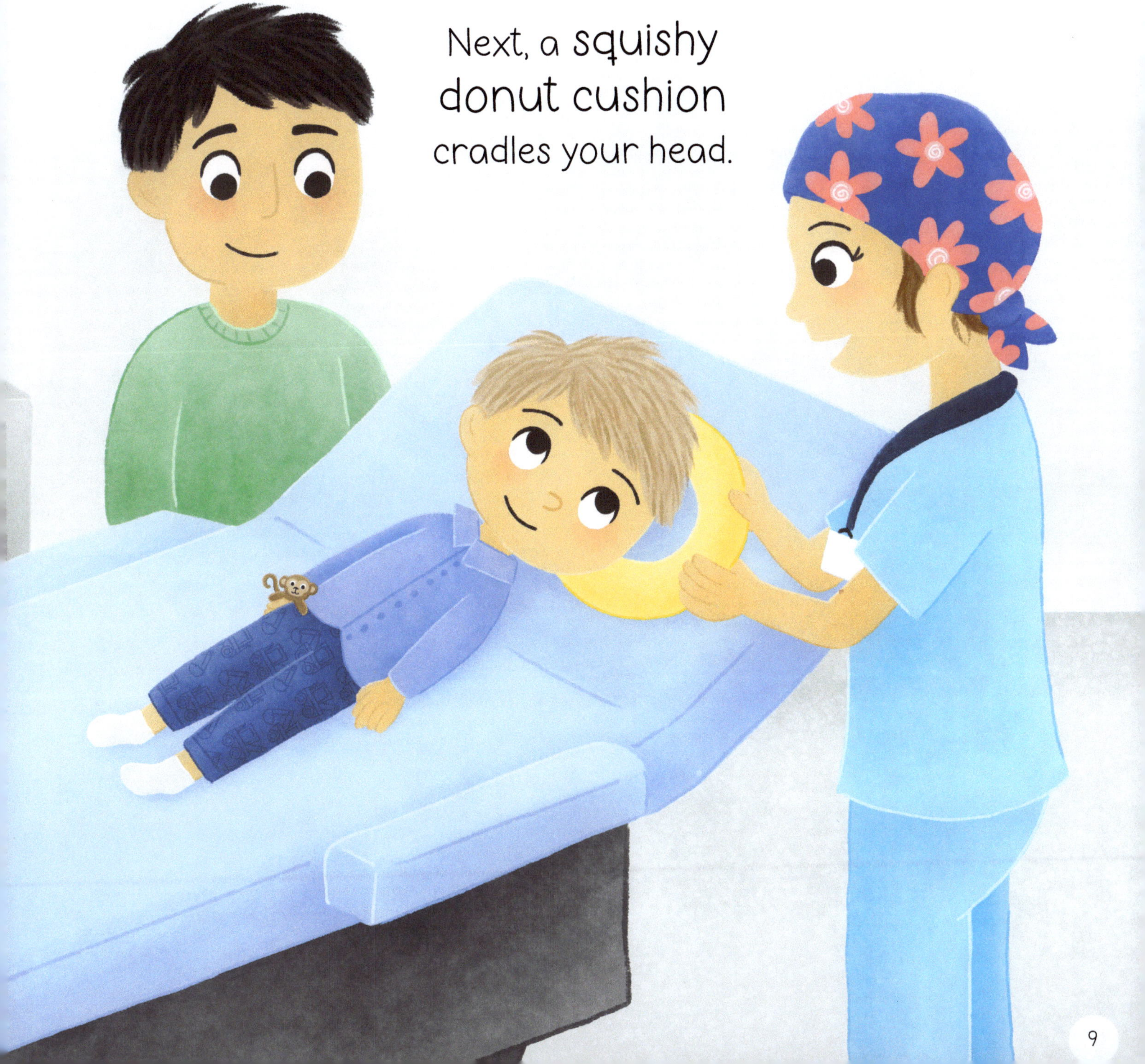

Some days, your bed wears a **sheet**,
Other times, a warm cloud wraps your feet!

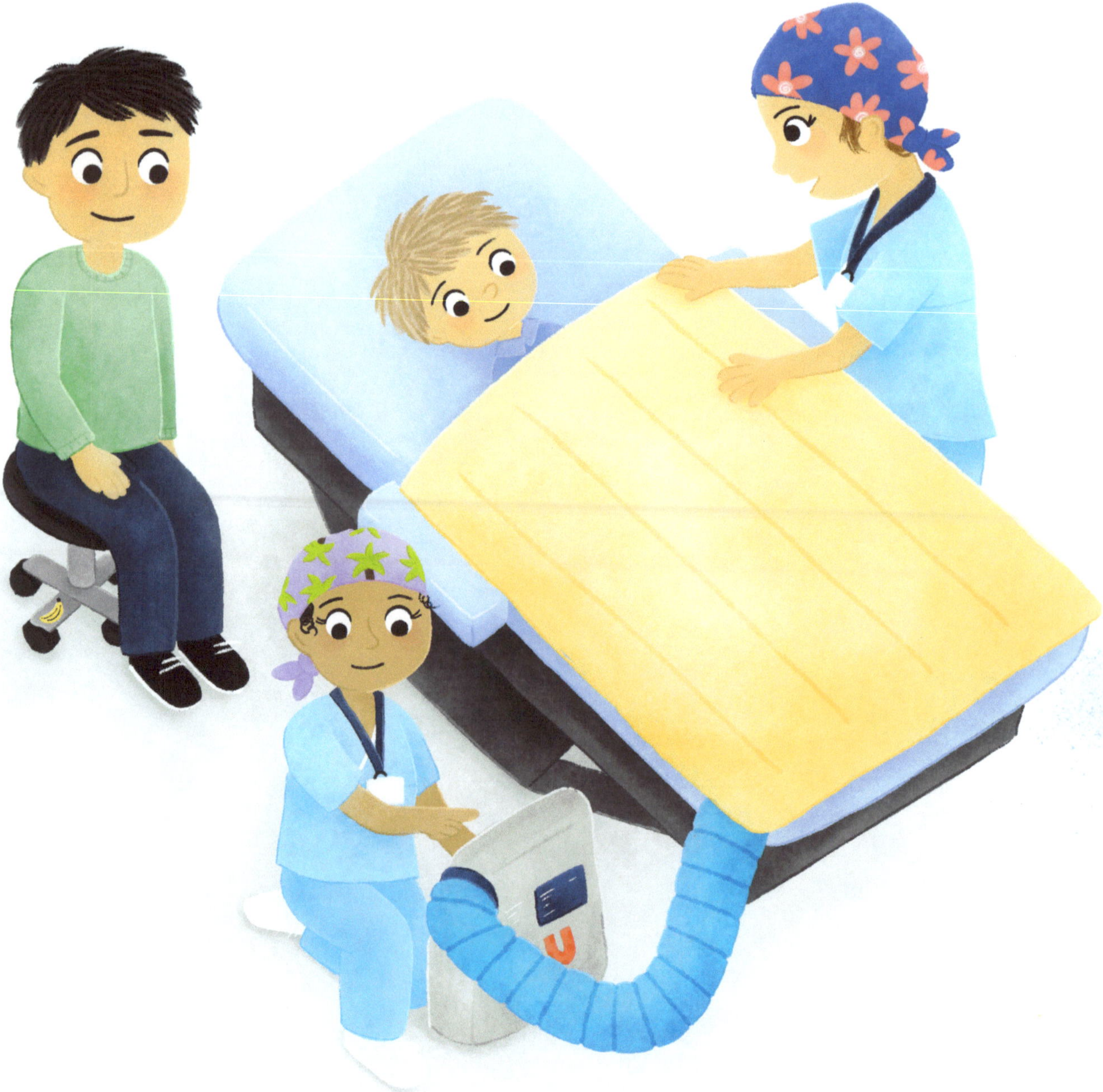

Snuggled up cozy from shoulders to toes,
You're ready to go where the **Dreamland** wind blows.

Next comes a fun surprise -
a green balloon!

You take a big breath,
and you're whisked away to the moon!

Then look to the corner,
with knobs and a screen
Is the curious, marvellous
Dream Machine!

You breathe in some **bubbles**
- wiggle your toes when you smell 'em!

They make you feel floaty...
a bit sleepy as well, then.

They drift through your mask,
gentle and slow,

And carry your thoughts to
where only dreams go.

Other kids get cold milk,
through a straw in their hand.
No bubbles for them,
but they're off to Dreamland!

Those children's dreams are full of treats,
where everything in Dreamland, is something to eat!

You'll soar for a while in
a world full of play,

Where animals talk and
wish you could stay.

But soon you whisper,
"I've got to go,"

There's somebody waiting -
it's time, now you know.

You open your eyes
and give a big grin -

Your adventure is over...

let the story-telling begin!

Secret Code Hunt Answers

You've done it - you've found every hidden polka-dot letter!

Now it's time to crack the code and discover your secret message.

Fill in each space below with the letter you found on the page number shown underneath:

WELL DONE!

You are now an official member of the

••••••	••••••	••••••	••••••	••••••	••••••	••••••	••••••	••••••
PG 7	PG 6	PG 17	PG 18	PG13	PG 14	PG 20	PG 12	PG 11

••••••	••••••	••••••	••••••
PG 19	PG 15	PG 10	PG 8

Real-Life Hospital Quest

When you visit a real hospital, keep your eyes open for these Dreamland treasures as they're hiding in plain sight!

See how many you can find with the help of your anaesthetist.

- Dreamland Doctor (anaesthetist)
- Surgeon
- Nurse
- Dream machine (anaesthetic machine)
- Donut cushion (head ring)
- Dreamland bed (operating table)
- Blood pressure cuff - gives your arm a hug
- Fancy theatre lights
- Sats probe (peg on your finger that listens to your heart beat)
- Vanilla milkshake syringe (propofol)
- Warm cloud (hot air warmer/ bair hugger)
- Green balloon (reservoir bag)
- Facemask
- Snorkel attached to your facemask (anaesthetic circuit)
- Yellow bottle of floaty bubbles (sevoflurane)

About the author

Lara Veronese is a specialist anaesthetist who helps little dreamers drift safely into sleep.

Originally from Cape Town, South Africa, she now lives in sunny Brisbane, Australia. After completing her anaesthetic training, she pursued a year of sub-specialist training in paediatric anaesthesia at Queensland Children's Hospital. Lara now has a mixed adult and paediatric anaesthetic practice and dedicates much of her time to teaching within the field of paediatric anaesthesia.

With a little imagination – and plenty of help from her own kids – Lara dreamed up the Dream Machine: a way to turn anaesthesia into an adventure filled with giggles, colour, and wonder. She loves spinning stories where each child helps shape the journey, choosing their own fun details before floating off into dreamland.

Her hope is that this book helps children feel brave and excited for their anaesthetic, and reminds grown-ups everywhere that courage often begins with a good story.

Tips for Parents

Understanding Perioperative Anxiety

It's natural for children (and parents!) to feel anxious before an operation. Hospitals can seem big and unfamiliar, and children may worry about the unknown. Those who have had prior unpleasant experiences with doctors or dentists are often more fearful. A little preparation, and lots of reassurance, can make a big difference.

Tips to Help Your Child Feel Ready for their Anaesthetic

1. Talk about it early, but simply.
Use gentle, age-appropriate language. Explain that the anaesthetist gives special medicine to help them go to sleep for their operation, and that you'll be close by before and after.

2. Read together or play pretend.
Books like *Road to Dreamland* or hospital role-play (using a toy stethoscope, mask, or doll) can help them understand what will happen in a fun, familiar way.

3. Let your child make small choices.
Children feel calmer when they have some control. Let them choose a comfort toy to bring, which pyjamas to wear, what they would like to eat after their operation or a favourite book to bring to read once they have woken up.

4. Stay calm yourself.
Children take their cues from you. If you appear calm and confident, they're more likely to feel safe too, and cooperate with the anaesthetic team. This is especially important during arrival in the operating room – your calm presence helps show your child that they are in good hands.

5. Bring comfort from home.
A favourite teddy, blanket, or sticker can make the hospital feel less strange.

6. Talk about "Dreamland."
Encourage your child to think about a fun dream or adventure they'd like to have – this turns the anaesthetic into something imaginative and fun, rather than daunting.

7. Ask questions.
Anaesthetists and nurses are used to helping families through this process. If there's anything you're unsure about, just ask!

8. Flag things early.
If you think your child may become particularly anxious or uncooperative before their anaesthetic, contact the hospital a few weeks before surgery and inform the anaesthetic team. This allows a thorough plan to be made for your child. It may include giving premedication (a mild sedative) or simply spending extra time helping your child become familiar with the environment and what to expect.

A Few Quick Tips for Anaesthetists

1. Offer as many choices as possible
Giving children simple choices helps them feel empowered and engaged.

I ask them to choose:

- where they want their dream to take place,
- an animal who will join them, and
- a snack they'd like to enjoy in Dreamland.

As they drift off, I tell a story using their choices – which keeps them focused, calm, and involved because it's their adventure.

I also let children decide whether they'd like to sit or lie down on the theatre table. In my experience, anxious children often prefer to sit, while calmer children are more comfortable lying down.

2. Timing and "Keeping it neutral"
I time the start of sevoflurane with the moment in the story when I mention a neutral smell – something without a strong positive or negative association.

Suggestions include: rocket fuel, car petrol, a yellow flower, princess bubbles, dinosaur breath.

Avoid promising specific scents like chocolate or banana – many children become disappointed if the smell doesn't match. Likewise, avoid negative references (like smelly socks!), as children will instinctively pull away.

Once the neutral smell is introduced, I shift quickly to link it to something positive and exciting:

"As you take a deep breath of the yellow flower, it makes you float... higher and higher... up the castle stairs... into a huge room filled with the most beautiful princess dresses! When you smell that flower, wiggle your toes. You decide to choose a sparkly pink dress and...."

This gives them something fun to look forward to – and makes them want to take that breath, to see what happens next.

3. Let one person do the talking
This is crucial.

Before induction, I explain to the anaesthetic nurse, trainee, and parent that it helps if only one person engages with the child during the process.

Too many voices can distract the child from the story and create overwhelm, which can lead to loss of cooperation. It can be useful to get the parent to have the task of holding both their child's hands, which provides comfort and keeps hands in a good safe spot.

4. And finally – have fun with it!
Children love silly stories, unexpected twists, and playful imagination. Don't be afraid to improvise, be animated, and enjoy the moment. When you're having fun, they feel it – and they relax..

www.ingramcontent.com/pod-product-compliance
Lightning Source LLC
LaVergne TN
LVHW070750090726
842905LV00011B/89
* 9 7 8 0 6 4 6 7 3 0 3 2 5 *